Bang!
Go All the Porch Swings

Bang!
Go All the Porch Swings

Poems By Grayce Scholt

iUniverse, Inc.
New York Lincoln Shanghai

Bang! Go All the Porch Swings

iUniverse books may be ordered through booksellers or by contacting:

iUniverse
2021 Pine Lake Road, Suite 100
Lincoln, NE 68512
www.iuniverse.com
1-800-Authors (1-800-288-4677)

Because of the dynamic nature of the Internet, any Web addresses or links contained in this book may have changed since publication and may no longer be valid.

The views expressed in this work are solely those of the author and do not necessarily reflect the views of the publisher, and the publisher hereby disclaims any responsibility for them.

Acknowledgments: Some of these poems have appeared in American Report, *The Blue Heron, The Christian Century, Michigan State University College Quarterly, Poet and Critic, The Red Cedar Review*, and *The Uncommon Sense*.

ISBN: 978-0-595-46234-6 (pbk)
ISBN: 978-0-595-90535-5 (ebk)

Printed in the United States of America

"… and all the while the chains are coming
all undone, the hooks on high are letting go
and bang! go all the porch swings
all across the earth,
clattering."

For Susan, for Jane
for all my dear ones
here and beyond ...

Contents

1

IN WAR IN PEACE

IN WAR IN PEACE

(1965)

In bed my blanket set at 7, I hang against a
sleepless sleep stretched crosswise on my mattressed tree
and from a thousand fathoms down the creeping comes, sometimes in rills of
wrinkling skin or wave or undulating gut that pitches,
rolls me like a leaf awash a-swirling in a concrete trough the kind that horses
sucked from long ago in front of the town hall at home.
Sick with outer sicker still with inner heat, I turn the blanket back to 3 and con-
cen-trate on sky that once and long ago upon my back I watched through green
trees by a stream that curled its way through silent Liedermyers' woods toward
sleep toward sleep toward *SPIN!* The dream uncurls and slams me upright in a
hole awash with worms and rot and from a thousand fathoms high the crinkling
comes comes down sometimes in cool festoons of tracer strafe sometimes in dust
my hands tear at tear at so hot so hot so *oh* and *ah* that
I can only retch and wet my pants again this time with blood
and *con-cen-trate* on one small patch of sky and it is blue beyond
the yellow smoke of Mekong fields of napalmed men and women boys and girls
and CONCENTRATE on sky and on one concrete
trough I dipped my feet in long ago and cry out
MEDIC MEDIC to an earless world that told us
long ago that
growing up
would
be
g
r
o
w
n
u
p
and
CON CEN TRATE and let my blood flood out
toward sleep toward silent night at home.

UNOBSERVED HE DIES

Unobserved he dies by eyes
that know no death. Ten water birds
fly up in fright of what his shadow
standing in the rowboat means;
they watch it twist and fall, unbalanced
suddenly as if in sleep or in
a wakefulness it can no longer bear,
plunge sidelong over, down and down.
One white bird flies away, but nine will settle soon
on nearby stumps unruffled, dark
against the coral Manistee at dusk.

From shore not far away two other eyes
are almonds in the reeds; the deer sees too
the drop into the coming night and kneels.
The sudden water beads it feels might be
the spray of shot the beast had one time felt
from such a shade. When only ripplings run away,
the red buck stands, draws his intended drink,
and veers toward forest brink.

From hill above a listless Holstein
separated from her herd and land
looks up and then behind her, half expecting
that the slap she hears is fecus dropping on the sand.
But feeling neither so compelled nor such relief,
she wraps her tongue again around
the clover head, the gentian leaf.

From far below two thousand eyes watch
as the body drops from dusk to dark,

watch red suspenders catch on roots
of death's enormous hook. One thousand mouths go
bump and bump, as if to taste the red wet wool
of shirt, the crystal watch, the finger's crook,
while child so stillborn in the gloom
goes undulating in death's private womb,

surrounded by the multitudes that unobserve
in undelivery room; they dart between his legs
in softly rolling swells
like fishes in the golden bowls
that exercise in castles, shells.

MASK-UNMASK

Really simple. Requiring
nothing but devotion to
because-I-did-not-care-not-dare-not-wear
(not well) not fare well at your
hands or feet or breast or
theirs or hers or his or
(there's the rub against the groin),
how-could-you-nevermind
you did and now there's nothing
(nada nada) naked nada
nodding in the shadowed
places of the years
and all because you opened holes
you had no right to look inside
and saw an excavated brain,
a pried up jaw from which words
ran out raw.

Simple. Nothing much required
to make a mask except
devotion to because-
how-could-you-nevermind-
you-did-you-did-mind-didn't-you?
Oh, it's nothing, really
nothing, why be
troubled
over
me.

FLIGHT INTO EYGPT

All this shouting *me! I!*
I am resurrection! Oh I am
light-and-fulla-beer-and-I-am-
slobbering-down-the-edges-of-my-beard-
you-know-I-sometimes-puke-into-the-toes-of-my-
brown-sandals-and-it-runs-out-the-heel-
I-trail-puddles-where-I-walk-of-bile-and-un-
digested-fat-and-shells-and-gas-and-napalm-whee
and-whee-and-wee-wee, *we.*

All across high heaven laughing rolls
while Harry Golden shakes his head
and lights another green cigar
and somewhere far away
Paul looks the other way and weeps.
Oh bleeding heart of Jesus in the five-and-dime
dry up dry up and crack before a poor soul
buys you takes you home to put beside her bed
while all the nuns move in and out their bodices
and all those bodies burn-like-hell.

If I were man enough I'd pop my fly
and piss across the universe.
I'd outen every
thing.

But no I hang a withered nipple down
in hopes a suckling pup might come.
You know the children all have fled and
Mary's gone to Bethlehem where tax is paid
for guns where all the counting's left uncounted

One where all the murderers have killed
the murdered Son and He, He stalks across the earth,
the earth as spectre floating
just beyond the tip of every touch
the lip of every kiss of every
undone doing
done.

GOOD FRIDAY

(For W)

Cruci
fix
ions
happen.
Stretched across
your rood
suffocating
in your
own white
blood,
I see you.
Christ.

Breast pierced,
poison drip-
ping through
thin tubes
descending
from somewhere
above.

I touch
your hair.
It sticks onto
my fingertips
as if it's
glued.

I touch
your hand.

Its parchment
taut across
your knobs
of joints.
No wonder
that you gave up
gardening.

I worry now
about that
pain.

You shrink
into your own
sarcophagus,
flesh to
stone.

I kiss you
one
last
time:
lips of ice,
eyes of fire.

Be care-
ful
on
the
road,
you try to say.

And that's
the end of it:

this way,
this day.

Outside the house,
three women talk,
a shadow falls across
the walk.
A small bird calls.

HAVING COME TO WHAT …

Having come to what I have become
I am what's gone, or almost gone,
like when our uncle tumbled from that cherry tree
in Carson's yard, the cherries he had picked
strewn on the grass (the doctor called it "stroke,"
my mother, "drunk").
He shook himself to death.

Like when old Mrs. Louck reached up to take
that mason jar down off the shelf above the stove
and showed my ten-year eyes her husband's yard-long
tapeworm she had saved from when he was alive.

Like when my buddy Curly crawled across the transom at the mill
and took two dollars from the till and was expelled from school.

And when my mother made a sandwich out of bakery bread
and gave it to the tramp who sat on our back porch
and ate. I watched him cry.

Like when the blind man that I knew told
how when as a boy a peach tree branch had snapped and
stuck him in the eye.

And when the hatchery man pulled out the lighted drawers
that stank from dying chicks
and flipped their floppy heads off
with his fingernail
and dropped them in a pail.

Having come to all I have become
such wisps that drift through dreams
are gone, or almost gone, not unlike

your dear face that's
    turned
        to
            smoke.

HEARING ALLEN GINSBERG

(Michigan State University, 1971)

Ah, Judas priest reincarnated
Walt-the-witman chants of oh my soul
my testicles. Old bearded solitary,
why of course you'd rise again
and sing your perfect wisdom
all across the windy weeds
of Wichita in dervishes in spiralings
from high Tibet to Independence Mo.
And don't fool us those mantras
swinging in their sino-Japanese
disguise are crossing Brooklyn ferries;
fairies, crones and alabaster knights
arise! it is your saintly sinner ringing
little finger bells *a-shake a-shake*
a-shake-shake-shake into the ear
of deaf America into the golden eye of
wheat vortex; it is the *ring a-ding*
a-ding-ding shaking down the conscience-
ness that these old states lost last year
was it Christmas riding towards L.A.
or 1865 or was it Hanoi
when the children's guts
exploded from the kiss
of Joe Smith's (bombardier) wet finger-
press or was it in a Mississippi swamp
in fire?

Oh king of May in Prague
on wet Long Island's shore
have pity pity, we who loaded down

with language guns and bread
can feel it too can feel and fear
and trusting emptiness as if it were
a god, must carry on in brutal silence
carefully and splendidly
must press must lean must shoulder wheels
that roll the glory guns into positionings
that point like black cocks
row on row ejecting toward the stars
one kind of dream, while you
the wounded prey that in us all
screams to be exorcized
throw back your bushy locks
and all together now
as if we were united states
cry out the wild in blood
in spit
in festerings
of love
the massive molecule,
the squeak,
the howl.

LANDSCAPE AFTER DOVER BEACH

Blisterdust sillsifts
from Chad from Malay rubble,
from bright Van Allen's belt
the wild mist falls,
sub-subscreams sing
unceasingly
at dusk.

Across the fields
the stubbles of our spires
stretch ten thousand miles,
in leafless ruin hang
bleeding choirs
where no throat calls.

On all earth's edges stands
the post, high-spiralling.
Oh lost, oh endlessly
in fierce erection
flooding sky
with old Cain lust.

O God I strain
to hear one pebble's grate.

No roar, no splash of old Aegean now,
no scrap of girdle furled to drape
the heart, no shore,

no naked night, no shingled seas
to summon up old Sophocles.

One rose-shot shred of paper swings,
a flag of simple then when armies
only ignorant clashed on plains by night
and true-to-one-another was enough
to salve the struggle
heal the fright.

A GUTTED FISH CAN SWIM

A gutted fish can swim, they say,
I've never seen it but I know
a headless rooster runs in circles
flapping wings until it drops.

One time I watched my
father strike the blow, the axe
was in his right hand; in his left
the wattle dripped down blood
and brains.

He spread the beak
between his fingers as if
listening for the crow
that still might come.
And then he
smashed it down.

ECLIPSE AFTER A DEATH

(April 8, 1993)

Even in the basement's dim
I see your notes: *Don't wash*
with colored clothes.
These socks are clean.

Outside, the shapes of trees
are black, their edges sharp,
their angles hard.

At feeders, pigeons, finches
peck. Two red squirrels
flash across the grass.

It is a dawn or dusk
to them, this light
between the worlds.

A letter came for you today,
not personal. For "medical"
it read. Long paid.

Last night Sierra Club,
the night before the Wildlife,
the night before—all calling you.

They say an annular eclipse
is on. The moon has found its way
across the sun. And not to look.

The rays, they say, will burn the eyes.
Oh, I'll not look-not look-not look.
I already know that ring of fire.

PROMISED LAND

Wedged into our public face
I find you stuffed beside me
in a toilet tank of dream.
I spill you out with one
quick handletrip and though
you fall into my laughing arms
I wake in terror wet and frozen
to the sheet.

Hung across our private lives
the flab of public chins hangs down
in everrolling folds a-slobbering;
strangled in such salivations that
I cannot spit beyond my lip
I cannot touch beyond a finger-
tip of fat my own
my own wet cheek.

O slit eyes saw and see no more
O crack ears heard hear nothing new
except for hammering of hearts
too small to pound the blood
through tons of flesh
through miles of capil-
laries inching life
toward dying glands
toward smothered
dreams that
choking drown in their own foul-O
down! down! down, go down.

Go down,
Moses.

Moses, Moses, let my people
let me
go.

AT THE MILITARY CEMETERY IN FLORENCE

(In memory of Lt. Deforest Buchman)

Five thousand crosses, marble, white
stretch across the grassy shroud
toward cypress trees, sharp sentinels
that guard the gate between the worlds
of life and death here in Firenze,
Italy.

I am remembering
that small graveyard where so long ago
my dad and I put flags on graves
on Decoration Day. And mother
on her knees beside the stones
put full blown peonies,
lilacs, purple, brought from home
into the pointed vases stuck in earth.

And then we'd leave,
go back to what we'd
come to know of holiday
and eat homemade ice cream
and watch the town parade
go down Main Street
go marching toward Flatiron Park
where some smart twelve-year-old
would shout out, "Fourscore-seven-years-ago ..."
and four old men would shoot old guns
and taps would drift from
down the street where a Boy Scout
bugler hoped his lip would hold

until a final dying note
could slip into the wind.

THE DEAD ARE DEAD

The dead are dead
we let them go.
Till closer, closer comes the dread
the letting of our blood, the flow;
while passings widen,
facts are known,
marrow hardens
in our bones.

We must let go
when summer's
blundered
into snow.

SO OUT OF SEASON, SNOW

"April is the cruelest month …"
                                    T.S. Eliot

So out of season, snow
has settled on the green hedgerow,
that only yesterday had felt
the kiss of April's glow.

Today the death
that's left of winter's breath,
the wind so soon forgotten
has revisited, all unbegotten
bringing its fierce treachery to earth,
its lechery of birth.

So out of season, cold
has settled on your lips,
that only yesterday had
felt the kiss of warmer clime,
has visited, unsought, has
brought the treachery of time
the scourge of old.

ELEGY IN SPRING

At our breakfast table
my coffee cup is empty,
our cat is pushing at my face,
I cannot read the news.

Through the window pane
I see our maple tree
weeping in the wash
of this May morning's rain.

Beyond, the lilacs that you planted
nod their heaving blossoms on the fence
as soft, voluptuous drops fall
through the Eastern light.

I hear you say
a rainbow must be
overhead
or in the West

but there's no sound,
no sound at all,
except the fall of
tears across the morning's
awful news.

BUILDING A NATIONAL CEMETERY

(Near Holly, Michigan)

Five hundred concrete vaults
stand at the ready, waiting
for the dead to come.
Trucks and cranes
move back and forth
around the lake,
across the hills dividing
cattails, bushes,
marsh grass, trees
into the grids where graves
will cross, recross
and cross again
and what is left of men
will press
into the opened earth.

Down the road
a single doe slips
through the brush.
She stops to watch,
steps backward, back,
and turns away.

SNAIL

No device to comprehend abyss,
elbow-anchored to the long-before
and ever-after-that
I slog in belly slime
across plateaus of now.

Yet sometimes
glassbound
how I know the weight
of my perpetual house,
how coiled for life
the cramp I feel
within the bowel,
awaiting that soft knife
that at the last explodes the dark
in warm emission
of the soul.

And then I think of all those pallid ones
who died puffpuffing sweeter more nor less
than I the plague of breath that turned them
on and off, and yes I wonder
at those all to come
those cheeks those lips
pushpushing death.

We touch
from first wet pass of gas
to cloud of cough.

DEAD DOGS

Dead dogs still wimper, whine at doors
although the doors are gone
the porch, the house, the town,
all that was so much
so everything that isn't now
except in dreams
that disappear when
daylight comes,

the light
that wipes
away
all tears, the
everlasting
tears.

EPITAPH FOR A LADY

(For GD)

You will not die. For when
the pedestal is empty
when the bust lies shattered
on the floor, I at least will kneel
will draw the velvet curtain
hung from rosewood turnings
taste the fume of rot leaves
burning in the yard.

The kingdom's come and gone.

Old servants all have scratched
on ivory feet toward graves,
old bones have fallen finally
to stony lions waiting at the gate,
gazelles are ash.

What's to endure?

A bird flies from a dying elm,
the leaves collide.
Their rattling runs around the world.

MANEUVERS OF SOME LATER WARS

I. *"The war to end war …"*

The spinning reels flicker, stop,
biplanes (prop to prop) hang
(nose to nose), enemies (*I/du-
you/dich)* in fierce repose.
WW eyes are burning!
Ace-high hearts are bold!
Whirrrr, the dim projector's turning:
silently we both explode.

II. *"The Good War …"*

From rubber raft I see
a blue stain sliding;
from broken sub below
your face is riding on the slick:
eyes are open,
lips are loose.
I lean out over you
(tooth to tooth)
of supernatural mile:
our death heads disap-
pear into the smile
of our first kiss.

III. *"… hearts and minds …"*

We fall across each other
near Saigon in the spring
not unlike lovers

rolling in embrace.
You draw your knife across
my jugular vein, I touch your face:
dying, with my careful gun
I shoot your balls off
one by one.

2

POSTCARD FROM A HIGH COUNTRY

POSTCARD FROM A HIGH COUNTRY

I am remembering on this page
a fine Tyrolean spring
another age, a hill we
struggled up to where
a crumbling castle stood
amid descending slopes
alive with greening wood,
of trembling shadows
where we lay
that kindest day.

Ascending to that rocky head
was our small way of holding
paper to the sun to see its
watermark. Fiercely young
we knew that we could live with lessons
or without.

Edging down the narrow route
we sent our postcard home:
a castle scene, wide-angle view,
but not of where we'd been
or what we knew,
or what we'd come to know.

"THREE SECLUDED ACRES"

(In Classified: *The Flint Journal*)

A county road, the realtor's sign,
stopping, backing up the car,
then stepping off one hundred feet
to measure what "four hundred
on the pavement" means.
Through thicket overgrown, waist high,
through goldenrod, through fern,
through popple dense, a scrub pine
here and there, some sycamore—
we fight our way into the ad's seclusion
toward a spot where light might fall,
where sun could shine
could penetrate, could pierce....
We try to see a summer house,
a weekend place, no more, ordering
this wild profusion.

Screened from all but barking dog
that's somewhere near, we try to think where
bulldozers could squeeze aside a space for drive.
We'd have to dig a septic tank, we say,
and well, lay down a concrete slab and raise a frame ...

We try to think of what it would be like
at night. We say we like it that no one is close.
We've driven all these miles
to find that no one is. But

even at this time of day the time of dark
appears some blacker than we'd thought.

And what about the shacks we saw along the way
the junked cars rusting in their yards
and whose dog keeps us well within his range
and why. We feel his eye.

I suddenly recall
a woman on the news last week
was bitten by a rattlesnake. Was it
twenty miles away?
or ten? or five?
A few are left in Michigan.

Fighting thick
mosquito swarms,
we turn.

Through ferns again,
through mushrooms,
toadstools big as saucers, plates,
some domed and yellow,
some as red as blood.
we weave. We push
through second-third-
fourth fall of leaves
across decaying roots.
to slide at last
into the ditch beside the road
and out. To touch at last
the pavement, hard, and
underfoot, and
good.

Inside, the car feels (though we
hadn't noticed it before) firm,
and rubber-sealed, safe.

We pull away. We say, "Well,
this place neared the mark."

Glancing in the rear view mirror,
I see a hound emerge from trees.
Barkless now he stands his ground
then drops beside the road into the weeds
to watch us disappear.

FAMILY CIRCLE

Around this
terry tablecloth
of cocks that strut
around we sit
spaced evenly
on all the spokes
of love's diameter
we face its hub
of spoon knife
fork its
cup its
breakfast plate
of blue egg
holding one gold
eye as yet
unbroken
in a soft
unending
shape of circle
holding love's
confinement in its
tender yolk
of dawn's commitment
one to
one
to
one
(around a
cloth of
cocks

forever
never
circling
more or
less.)

FOR HONEY BOY, A DOG

His golden hair streams out behind his hocks
in aureoles of light, as crashing through the grasses
toward the shore, he splashes into swirls of lake,
and stops.

With forepaw raised, his gaze intent,
he bites relentlessly the glaze of light
as if his life depended on the catch of
one small fish.

And then he stops. He whirls around
as if surprised by his own wish
and gallops shoreward shaking
his bright diamond gifts all over us,
his eyes aflame
with love.

FISH STORY

Slip-into-me, cries fish to water, and out.
    I gill you.
Slip-into-me, cries water to fish, if out
    you die.
If I run-through-run-through-run-through you,
    I kill.
(Fish drown, you know that?)

Isn't it curious that love that hangs
    too near the water lays its sharpened
shadows on the pond like oblique swords
    or words? Shadows drown in dark, you
know, and dark in light.

Slip-into-me, says day to night.
    Slip-into-me, says night to day.
If I run-through run-through-run-through you,
    days drown in breath.
(But that you knew.)

PROGRESS

I. Cutting Trees for Another Expressway

With me I die and that
is nothing at the last,
like trees first topped
then ground by gnashers,
whining growlers screaming guts
across the neighborhoods
at noon.
      Limbs fall first
then shredded, hauled,
hauled away on yellow rigs
that hold hard-hatted drivers
with no face at all;
trunks go down at last
and blank wide eyes of stumps
stare open to the sky.
      By and by small birds come down
and pick at here and there,
at bugs and ants that search for sap
that has nowhere to go.
Finally the shredder comes for
even stumps.
      Last birds go.

II. Blacktopping for Another Parking Lot

With trees I die and we, we
all die out, having fallen
on asphalted spring; no more
to tremble to the rage of wind

and wing. We die to need,
our seed a double-shafted sprite
that hovering in its flight
must drop at last on pavement
burning, burning,
sealed tight.

OUR OLD MATH

Adding up the sum
I find the multiple of one
divided by a zero
equals what I know of you.

And what you know of me
divided equally
remains the multiple of one;

thus, Total Sum
of one plus one
is in that plus
that equals us.

IN DEMELS

(Vienna, Austria)

In *Wein-Wein-nur-du-alein*
where black-green table tops
are wet from sparkling water
set for chasing *torte,*
schlag, cafe mit schlag,
schiffe, chocoladen,
schlag und Kaisertorten,
schlag, und cafe gold, und
schlag mit schlag—

while two *dunn dame*
slightly old lift
two white cups
between their talk
while all around them
mirrors reflect more mirrors
and from the ceiling's
great glass curve the
chandeliers glow bright
with globs, *mit* globs of
schlag, mit chocoladen,
torte, Kaisertorten,
schiffe, schlag mit
golden *schlag* that drips
like *licht von himmel*
on sticky lips,
on silver spoons.

SQUIRREL

Be careful of that squirrel you said
and you were right, I should be. But it's been
flashing through my dreams and rumpling sheets
down all these years until I swear
I feel its fur beside me on the bed.
Sometimes I hear it scuttling deep
inside the walls of this old house
scritching, scratching like an itch
I can't quite reach.

Of course I've set a trap, a fine wire trap
baiting it with that same fruit that flattened
Eden long ago. But that old squirrel's too sly
to come to such an end
when it can come and go at will
through openings it remembers well,
its jaw aflame with nuts
its paws still groping
for a nest.

HEARING A BLOCKFLØTE IN WIEN

A tune runs through my night
as old as love, as sure as death
and dances there along the bone
to flutter finally in shapes of breath
that drop pure bells upon the city snow
outside. Darkness hugs our pane.

Inside, the soft wild sings.
Bright, your rose pipe trembles lightly
in our tiny room, touches, tips at last
the free thing, sends my poor heart
spilling wide across this box of light
that someone far across the river sees
as a speck in the night
in a roofbank flat
against the sky.

A RIDE IN THE COUNTRY

We roll between the dying elms
on wheels forever separate
spinning on the axis of our earth
sideways together and yet not together
through the night,
           on gravel road
that leads us orbiting a whitefaced lake
that must from distance of perhaps a loon
hang like a moon itself against
the black of wood;
           like children,
starting, stopping, darting
now and then ahead, we play
at what we both know is a joke and yet
we've come somehow to cherish
that which holds our axle-yolk
apart and not apart here in our dark,
or so we say;
           and yet if unicycles
were a practicality, a mode,
I swear I'd choose to be transported
one on one with you
along most any road.

THE HARP TEACHER'S DAUGHTER

Grace Wiedermann was made to practice
till blood oozed from her fingertips,
till Papa said *genug!* *(*enough)
but just for *jetz*! (now)
Or so I heard when I was ten.

I dreamed of Grace last night
I saw her blood drip down
the thinest strings, then
cascade down the thick bass cords,
in bright red rivulets
that splashed on pebbles,
beaches, rocks,
that stained the marsh grass,
cattails, docks
till stream was pink,
the lake red raw
while Vater nodded
ja, ja, ja!

meine tochter,
ja!

EXCOMMUNICATION

Beside you in a county park
we fight off May,
its honey load between us
like a hive at point of drip.

Sweetly sick we speak
of icy lives that will not melt
in hottest sun (the code unbroken)
taking care to shape what will suffice
to shun the blue (the word unspoken)

trampling as we make escape
sweet william in the leaves below,
ankle deep in winter's cuff,
lips still mouthing snow.

HALF IN LOVE WITH BILLY

Half in love with Billy, Stanley, Merwin, W.S.,
Hopkins, Pinsky, Levertov, and all the rest.

But so in love with Emily, Emily in white
bending over dashes in the dim lamplight

listening to a fly buzz, surmizing horses' heads
stashed away in deepest drawers, perfect silver beads,

syllables so frozen they shudder in the gloom
suffocated in the air of sealed tight tomb.

Where was resurrection? Not for her to know
buried in New England winter, pale lips breathing snow.

SPELUNKING

I would have said that
we had studied openings.
It was our course, exploring
cave and cove with torches and without;
on thread as tough as rope, we traversed
distances as steep as time across
abysses black as space and cold.

I would have said that
we had broken rock together,
mallet striking bright quick flicks
that opened ancient fins and wings,
that we had run our fingertips
across the ages, touching flesh
that dropped a million years ago.

But now I know the distances,
were dead as webs that bound us
separately, that held us fast
within the tomb, were voyages
beyond the moon.

I would have said that
we had studied openings,
but found instead
ourselves the relics
sealed within the ruins.

LOAVES AND FISHES

(A poem for my unborn child)

My father's folding and unfolding his old hands,
fingering fragments of a time I never knew; without her
deaf, much deafer than before, he sits in yellow light,
almost blind and white; around him stand their
trellises, wallpaper thin, that shut the now without,
the then within.

We had touched once.
One August dusk our rowboat
drifted onto pond lilies so thick
we could not move, nor drop another
line to fish, nor care to.
He told me of the tanglement
below the boat, how lilies grew,
how deep it was, and see that bird
there on the shore—a heron! Blue.

He stood, the heron flew in
slowly beating flaps it rose
toward heaven. And then he turned
his back to pee across the stern
of our old boat. Into the evening sun
his water flew, a fountain of himself
he threw with much delight.
He sat again this time to sing.
I hear his voice roll yet
across that Mud Creek night,
though I forget his tune.

Finally he pushed us off
our flower bar, and I rowed home.

Our catch was hardly worth the fire,
two little fish, bullheads at that
and skinned with pliers.
With bread she'd baked,
our trinity complete. In love's
old agony of that communal feast,
we ate the holy flesh and blood
of parent, child.

I finger now the times you never knew,
struggling how to not observe the un-born you.
For I could never send my monumental
argument into the sun, for us no heron flew,
nor could I sing one song, nor give you one thing
to recall—not two small fish.

Now I have come too far to get hung up
on lily pads. Yet, the dream persists:
Help me, my child, to row us home,
Child? Night insists

EXHIBITION

Late from the killing jar
speared to the navel
this fly dried
gut gone.

Eyes unseeing
eye to eye
reflect the
countless me's

reflecting even one
that could not
swat ...

PRELUDE TO SPRING

A sparrow
under the eaves
with wings brown-flecked
like the specks
in your irises,
lies
supremely
still.

Death, a cruel
and stiff-winged thing,
exercises
under eaves
even as
buds
begin.

CARESS

May apples grow
in our dark woods
in our small clearing.

All around wet sunshafts
ravel down in cylinders aglow
with grains that rise and fall
(a glancing pain).

Remembering well that
silently you said
this ground was surely
where the child Eve
awoke to Adam first

and I remember all the rest.

Not daring now as then
to stop the rich contagion,
I stand in velvet penetration
once again. In wild
ascent/descent
without one bee
I swear that I could
fertilize this earth
of trees.

But only human,
fuller than I've ever been
of love's distress, today
I turn and walk (right-thigh-rubbing-left)

caress (left-thigh-rubbing-right)
away.

ON SEEING A NEWS ITEM

From the column's half-tone gray
blank eyes stuck just below the bangs
look, incline a bit
as if they had been pasted down
by one expertly grim
in not quite photographic art.
Black type above, below,
tells of her timely death:
eighteen, head-on,
long lids drawn down at last.

Oh, I remember her:
remedial in English
but without remedy in language, life,
enrolled in syntaxes far slipperier
than writing one's own name (a task),
engulfed in dictions
too demanding to express
foul weathers, fair,
life at impoverished home,
or fear of Y-room nights
without an ear to hear,
but without even hate.

Those eyes could only
as she hurt us both
find pity then in mine;
blank lips could only
speak in gray
of what she felt
if she did feel,

of what she knew
if oh indeed she did know
anything at all.

She saw that day some kind of pain.

I saw her eyes were two blue wafers
on a plate.

Across my desk, she pled for life
that she could understand
so it would understand
what she would understand if ...

Vacuous child, trembling.

Head-on, the wafers touched the chaliced wine.
By some profound intinction all came clear.
Her knowing now is my unknown.
I plead before the altar
of her death.

FIRST GRADE

(Remembering Mrs. Bense)

While she rubbed our poor
child's hands to life,
we heard our teacher saying
frozen, blue. We gawked,
we wondered at the words,
at the smell of lilac rising
from the dark cloak room.

And then she came, Our Teacher,
flinging long arms over us;
dropping from her fingers' spread,
the sparks of spring …

Wriggling, ducking, laughing as
the petals sprinkled over us, as
love was sprinkled over us,
the incense from the ashes of
that burning bush
in bloom.

WATCHING A MAMMOTH'S SKULL BEING WASHED

Yesterday
impacted in primordial clay,
in blue-gray womb, stillborn,
twelve thousand years
you trembled only
at great mother's turn.

Today
extracted, hosed, and scrubbed,
in vacant stare a heavy deathhead
spilling mud across the vinyl squares;
no spinal fluid, blood
to stain the laboratory floor,
no trace of grass no man will see
still clings to gray incisors (scored
like Ked soles from mishapen dyes),
no spittle dropping from the jaw,
no tears, no eyes.

Old muncher, tusked, and woolly-curled,
twice afterbirthed to worlds
profoundly cleaved by fire and ice,
forgive this rough device of ours.
We leave you shortly, packed in clay
more strange than yours,
awaiting some bright shovel's probe
across our bones' death-heavy load,

deep on our Barkowski farm,
along our Duffield Road.

EIGHT O'CLOCK CLASS

(After assigning Gerard Manley Hopkins' "The Windhover")

Shackled to the podium
the albatross of English lit
around his neck,
he lifts a balding eye
toward all the faces,
takes the roll: Adams,
Ash are gone, Helms
and Steiner too will miss
the windhover this
morning-minion-bright
will miss the sight
the sound of wimpling wing
astriding under tiles dead-
white, acoustical, will never
know His fluttering toward
fluorescent tubes nor see His
plume askance His undone
buckle buck, will never feel
His firefall-flipflop-neckbreak
on gray bricks of glass
that hold these halls of learning up.

O vacant chairs and still
more vacant eyes. Sheer plod
makes plowboys without down,
no sillions shine, old embers
gold ungashed grow dim.

"This morning," pleads the bleak-
blue voice, "we will begin ..."
(O Christ Our Lord) again.

COMMENCEMENT

Into each other's state we pass,
showing visas, paying coins;
at this suspension, at this gate
our countries meet
though no lands join;
arched across the boundary flood
our height be noted only
that its cloudy tower tops
the pilings deep beneath the sea.
You come to me.

And so we pass,
we flow across a bridge that's hung
on silver wires beneath
a sky of glass.

We have become
the going, and the coming
and the road that has no turning
on the no return to home.

EDGES

I waded Muddy Creek,
fished the broad Maumee
and I knew Erie's pranks:
her flattened cheek
her frothy foam
against her banks;
I stood beside her eye
unblinking in night sky
and watched the reds and greens
go winking toward her
retina of shore.

I knew some waters
long before I saw Atlantic gray.
But with that first intake of spray
a rising in me, in itself a sea
broke fortress continent
and fired in me
the utter discontent
of sweet discovery.

YE WATCHERS, YE UNHOLY ONES

Tonight the stone-faced moon
gessoed against the cobalt sky
is alabaster bright, is beaded calcite
brush-daubed onto velvet folds
that roll around the universe.

Or like a marble, limestone white
a metamorphized glowing taw
a shooter shot from god-child's hand
encircling what we know of hell,
the marcacite we fear from heaven.

Or like a vast cyclopean eye,
a vitreous light that opens once
then closes, closes, closes tight
into our night.

EQUINOX

The equinox has come
a fall day oddly warm,
the gulf stream having snaked
across the weather map
and dropped its blue snow
on the North.

But this warm blessing still abounds
for us, so out of season, out of sync—
I should be raking leaves and covering beds
and hanging storms, instead

I watch a frenzied sparrow flutter
in the bird bath drumming wings
that send bright sparks of fire
across the grass. Though bird and I
know well that this day cannot last,
we celebrate the interim.

WRITING ON A WORD PROCESSOR

A poet ought to be
inspired by a WP
and grateful
writing as he does
on specks, on specks of—
no, on micro-specks of
dust, no, no, on
micro-dust that's
settled on a chip,
a micro-macro mite
that's come cavorting
through the deep
celestial seas
of galaxies,
come bumping,
thumping off of
planets, stars,
to be transformed
in brief electronic
thrusts into a poet's
thoughts, words,
sighs,
that only now appear
so fleetingly
on his dark screen
as light.

3

CHAINS OF BEING

CHAINS OF BEING

The lips, the vessel photograph
shows me to me. I see my mother
in the parted smile, winking
from across these thirty years
of black-white death.

        ****

Behind newspapered windows how we bottled beer
in basement under forty watts: first
he sucked it up into a hose then spit the
first foul on the floor, then more and more
came brown and right until we'd filled each one,
till hose had schlupped and that brown crock
stood empty smelling like it had been sick
while bottles all erect their heads afoam
stood leaking bubbles on cement
awaiting caps.

        ****

Chattering,
two salts of earth sit on a porch swing
weaving 'twixt the old morality
and all the while the chains are coming
all undone, the hooks on high are letting go,
and bang! go all the porch swings
all across the earth,
clattering.

A MIDNIGHT SWIM

I only saw you drunk that one time
coming from the boat plant picnic.
You were driving, laughing,
mother crying, crying you-will-kill-us.

In the back seat on the mohair
I was fingering it first one way
then the other, smoothing, smoothing it,
trying not to hear you, hear her,
trying not to notice how the car was
flinging me against the one door
then the other, swinging side to side
across the gravel loose and bumpy
trying hard, hard to remember how
you held me tight last night
how we hung onto the rowboat
splashing through the water,
one hand locked onto the boat
the other wrapped around your shoulder
clinging to the rough strap
of your bathing suit.

Through all my
stinging nose
my aching throat
I heard you singing,
heard Doc Heller singing
as he rowed us through the dark,
and just like that I felt the bottom

felt the beach and
felt you kiss me

as you let me go.

WAITING FOR A WALTER DRAVES

Spiraea flakes fell
lightly in my dark.
Cool, my cramp of house
hid my small body
in its box of green and
I became a nested bird,
a resting bug, a worm inch
inching up a stalk,
a clod, a broken brick,
all, all unmoved,
unreconstructed.

Every dream ascended there,
descended without finger lift.
Every ambush planned
and executed died within those
hours of births and deaths.

I sat through solitudes
as thick as those green bushes.
towering. I waited
for a Walter Draves.

And when he came pumping, pumping
in his chair, his cap aslant
across his droop of face,
I thrilled to hear
his whistle-breath,
his call for me to come,
to sit upon the step,
to face his mute mouth, grunt,

his pain. I knew what Walter
wanted.

(Like ice cream cones
he waited for uptown.
If someone bought him
strawberry, his fat hands
stuffed the cone into his maw,
his old cap falling even lower
as he drooled his nodding thanks,
his benefactor walking off
not looking back, half guilty
for the gift and half astink
with nickel's worth of pride.)

I knew this manlump stuffed between two wheels
wanted me to talk, to sit beside him
filling his thick maw of ears
with what we children did and said
and who won what and lost and what
we thought and what he'd never
hear us say in all his life to him.

And all the while,
white blossoms fell
into my dark.
I folded
outside in
and never
moved.

When at last he pumped away,
I crashed through branches,
petals flew. And when I knew

he still could hear my faintest call,
I cried his name: "Walter!
Come back. We'll play!"

But when he turned
(oh splendid game!)
I stood full view
and waved,
and ran away.

I CAN ALMOST SEE YOU

I can almost see you
with the nineteenth century
sitting on the shelves behind
your shoulder: Dickens,
Trollope, Lewis Carroll
all arranged just so.

I watch you work,
so concentrated, fused
to what it is that lies
before you on your
shadowed desk.

I sit in sunlight,
with my coffee cup before me
full,
half-full,
so empty,
fingering toast.

I plead for one more glance
before you fade, before you pass
into the bindings, covers, spines
of what is gone, of what it was
so long ago, so ordered

so arranged
that we could not believe
could not imagine how it
ended, having yet to read

the final pages of our story's
book.

ASKING ALL THE QUESTIONS

Asking all the questions
staring at a box of salt
so long ago, listening to our mothers
saying what-will-happen-will,
oh-what-will-happen-what-before
this-box-of-salt
is-all-used-up?

You and I, Louise
and Clara, Gladys, Min,
Lucille bending
in our kitchens,
bedrooms, basements
turning tons of
wet clothes, dry clothes,
cups and saucers
forks and spoons and
hamburg, hot dogs
smoothing, squeezing
moulding into doughy lumps
that never make themselves
before they smear and want
re-kneading, stick and want
re-shaping, want
re-newing, shaping, kneading
endlessly on kitchen counters
every
where.

Questions, all the questions
flowing out across the floors

toward four corners bright with clean,
curling there like kittens watching,
waiting for the mouse they know
is there, but will not run.

DANCE FOR A DEAD PRINCE

His name was Witt.
We called him Half and Nit and Dim.
His mother called him Jack.

The family lived in one continual snit,
"Feeble-minded," said his card.
Was not his last name Witt?

At ten, his brother drowned, his twin.
He could have saved him if he'd tried.
The whole town called him Half and Nit and Dim.

His mother cried and finally cracked.
He peddled papers from a cart.
She'd called him Jack.

Alone, at fifty five, in some blue fit,
he smashed the wagon up and jumped
(his last name Witt)

exactly where his brother'd drowned, his twin.
No longer half or nit or dim
(his mother'd called him Jack)
he had paid his brother back.

MEN DESCENDING

I never think about the thirties
without remembering men
descending stiffly from the boxcars,
winter light upon their single face
screwing mouth into the bleary questions:
am I? where have I been? will be? when?

They stretch and scratch beside the cars
the raw wind catching now and then the nogood
news that crackles from the doors
thrashing wrappings down and under far across
the yard; they stand in knots as if they're
frozen, stuck to iron.
                              Some strike
the houses near the tracks to ask for coffee, sugar,
could they shovel snow; some walk off heavily
along the line toward camp where if they are in luck
a spire of smoke is rising from a fire beneath a pan.

They disappear across the earth by day
until the dusklight grows. Then it's as if
a silent trumpet blows that brings the groups
or singles filing from the hills, carrying papers,
clutching jugs. They slip again into the switchyard
open-close the iron grills of wheat cars partly filled
or empty caverns cold and still and enter in
to wait for light.
                              I think about that blackness
remembering too the silence that the night provides
for one who woke, who journeyed into deepest dream:

Clang! the doors fly open, drop him on a golden street
where on a screened-in porch she stands
waiting in the sun, where she,
her arms outstretched to him,
watches his ascent
toward home.

FOR AN OLD WOMAN, DYING

I never saw it, yet I see
the wraith she was that fled
across the meadow near the house,
her mother half her size smash-
smashing down the buggy whip.
I hear the cries, the Luther-fury
foaming from her mouth
her hausfrau shame: a daughter-runaway-
a-Frenchman-hired-man-to-blame—
crack! CRACK! *O Gott,*
her Lily in white calico,
the dress she'd made by lamplight
not for this, not this.

Under blows that though they missed their mark
still burned. They lurched across the bayou bridge
that linked the bank to bank.
And then *die Mutter* stopped
to lay the whip across the farthest plank:
Meine tochter, do not cross this
if you do not mean to stay!
She turned away.

When Lily saw the whip, a serpent
on the board, she flailed her arms
against the sky in blasts of strength
until she sank against the marsh
collapsing into cattail rank.

She stood at length
and gathering what was left to be,

she took his medal from her throat
and found a stone.
that would forever mark,
be monument
for her alone.
She kissed the spot
as she had kissed his lips, his hair.

She buried blue St. Anne
and left her there. Then

back to where the black whip lay,
she coiled it on her arm,
and headed home.

Her mother never looked to see
who opened up the door a crack,
said only, "Pigs need slop. Be quick."

High behind the kitchen door
Lily hung the whip.

Inside the barn,
her Jacques being gone filled up
the nave like fresh green hay. At length,
beneath the loft where they had lain,
she slopped the hogs again.

I never saw it, yet I saw it in
those last days of her life—
running, wringing hands
until they bled, cringing,
crying, still she fled,

flailing feet on wheel chair rest,
blue St. Anne upon on her breast.

A WINTER DEATH

Ice chinks kiss the window pane—
the frozen sash forced up.
Down in the street they shout,
"Come home. She's dead."

Through blinding snow the stiff sedan
goes bouncing over icy ruts.

Inside the living room
I see him staring, blank,
as if his eyes are stuck
on where he saw them
struggle with the body bag
so black, so heavy
down and round the
landing steps
and out the door.

Tears will come
but not tonight,
snow too fresh,
ice too cold.

TWENTY-THREE!

(For my sister in her dementia)

"Twen-ty-three, three, twen-ty-three."
She's sitting at the table,
whispering the words,
her old hands folded reverently
as if in prayer.
And then a shot tears through her brain,
her hands are fists and she is shouting,
pounding out the syllables of
"Twen-ty, twen-ty, twen-ty-three!"

We look away. Her kitchen's filled
with strangers, ugly strangers,
daughter-sister strangers standing
at her stove, her sink.
"Oh, twen-ty, twen-ty, twen-ty three!"

Dear God.

We chop, we stir, we move
between the cupboards, counters, tables,
laying out the knives and forks,
cups and saucers, plates and spoons,
touching her thin shoulders,
stroking her gray hair,
trying not to hear,
to see her eyes so wide
so wild. She stiffens, spits, she screams
her only solace: *"Twenty-three!"*

until the whole house shivers,
shakes our quaking hearts.
And we sit down to eat.

INSTRUCTIONS FOR MY DISPOSAL

(After reading a description of cremated remains in a funeral director's pamphlet)

Drop at least
one pinch of my leftovers
into the urn at church,
just in case …

Then make a pouch
of my old bones, all pulverized
"like sand, like crushed seashells"
and dump the sandy part
where we sat long ago
in that old leaky rowboat,
scraping bottom
raising little clouds of earth
frightening fishes
darting toward
the river's shore.
And take what's left
on to the coast.

But there's no hurry.
You can wait till you
go East one day, some summer's
day or sometime in the fall
when you are willing
to endure the long turnpikes
the snarl of Boston, bridge to Cape,
and follow route Six A through Sandwich,

where we stopped to
ooh and aah at glasses in a window
where the woman told us
"Lamplight's best,
to show their reds."

Then drive past Dennis,
Brewster, Mass. and even on to Orleans;
but when the elbow crooks
toward North, stop ...
Stop at Eastham.

Yes, at Eastham,
at that cottage where we felt
the wet seawind
and worried if the septic tank
was way too full to pee in,
where the propane gas went *whoosh!*
every time we lit the stove.
Yes, it was at Eastham
where we tramped the sharp salt marshes
when the ebbing tide
left thick brown brine,
for giant gulls to swoop at,
feasting on the live
things left in pools.
It might be there at Eastham
where you put my seashells
on the rounded rocks
while white gulls swarm
and cry and cry.

Or better still, go on
to where the days begin,

to Provincetown, to
where those wretched Pilgrims
first touched foot
believing they'd
found home.

Then, if you will, please scatter
what is left of me
in that forgiving foam
that pardoning sea
where all beginnings
ebb and flow
in perpetuity.

CANCER

My father said he knew he'd die of cancer,
hanging like a festering brick
inside his bowel, that bag of pus.
He spent his lifetime
fighting, fighting it.

He'd pack the family up
and drive those fifty miles to where
a clinic did colonic irrigation
Monday, Wednesday, Friday
while we waited in the car.
When he came out he'd say
he guessed he'd fooled that cancer
one more time.

But after that it was bran flour,
and oats and beans, cascara drip and teas,
psyllium seeds and nuts and prunes
and oh yes, water too, lukewarm
with Epsom salts, two pints
from his green mug
upon arising everyday.

Till finally at seventy
a doctor wondered if it might be,
yes perhaps, just maybe—he'd
lost weight—and yes, an X-ray
showed a mass, a tiny mass ...
excised.

He lived another long six months
until one night he failed to stop

his car. It eased onto the highway
as a semi-truck bore down.

He fooled it one more time.
The cancer cured.

JAPAN!

"Hey, Ma, we got Japan!" He'd laugh and clap his hands
("That's nice," she'd say, and go on working at the sink)
or Paris or Berlin. Or sometimes on another band
we'd hear the state patrol say, "There's a bull loose
on Route 2 by Toussaint Bay. I need some help!"
Once when a plane flew over we could hear the pilot
say he saw that arrow pointing East,
that arrow painted on the basket factory roof.

But how he loved to tune the short wave band
that pulled in stations far away, sometimes.
The Philco had a lighted dial
so I could read the names of cities
if I looked real close—London, Rome
and some I don't recall, but Tokyo
was best.

(This was before the War of course,
and I was ten years old. I read the names
out loud to him.)

Then through the static's *cric-a-crac*
he'd shout "We-got-Japan-by-God!"
and how he laughed.

I read the cities' names to him because
when as a boy while walking through an orchard
close behind his dad, a peach tree branch
had snapped out from his father's hand
and punctured his left eye. And then infection spread
to his right eye. And he was blind.

I studied that black hole and tried to think
what it was like to have a hole like that one in his eye,
to have a hole like that one in my eye.

I asked him once if it was dark inside.
"Not black," he said, "just gray."

And then, "I don't remember what a day
looks like, or night, or grass or sky
or blossoms on a peach tree branch in sun.
I don't remember....
Ma! We got Japan!
And there's a bull loose
on Route 2. Remember when
we heard that plane?
and the pilot saw that arrow
on the basket factory roof?
He saw it pointed East, why
he was going to Tokyo
by God to Tokyo!
And we have it got it, Ma
right here!

Can you believe it, Ma?
We got Japan!"

RAILROAD BRIDGE

Running toward the river, grasses parted
underfoot like knives thrown quick
beneath our feet. (You never could step on a snake
not even if you tried but oh I never tried, not me.)
I lifted feet as high as hell and ran like it
to get to that forbidden tub and to the joy
of pushing off into the coming dark.

Joe, Jack and I would bail and bail
and Ha! those oars, one split, the other short,
but once aboard that rub-a-dub we'd row,
and swirl in circles, each one worse at rowing
than the one before.

In fifty strokes or so we'd round
the Cape of Hope and head toward
bridge abutment on the Wheeling line,
tie up, climb onto it, and dip our toes
into the lead of dying day. Not much to say,
we'd sit in coral light and swat.

We'd sit there till the eight-o-two was due.
And then we'd hear her. Trembling, we would drop
down far beneath the ties to wait. And she would
come and come until she struck that bridge
right down to its bed rock.

With hope yet fear that one day they would find
us squashed beneath her wheels, we knew
somehow we'd live to tell about the monster's pass,

to tell just how the cinders spit and
kissed the riverskin.

At last, unbloodied, whole, we'd board again and bail,
and by the Greatest Circle Route known
then to man, somehow we'd beach, sprint through
the marsh, and still alive and undiscovered,
hightail home.

FARM AUCTION

Her quilts are spread across the grass,
embroidered towels stitched patiently
in white Aladdin light
stacked beside
half-rotten whiffle trees,
hog hooks, milk cans,
one rocking chair,
two shotguns, both
twelve gauge.

It's good they're dead.
Her linens hanging
on his hoes and rakes—
who would have thought
that such a thing
could be.

He would have turned his head away
and walked toward field;
she would have dropped her eyes
and pursed her mouth.

I should be buying just because
they made these things
they handled them,
because they had their
smell on them, their touch,

but I've no taste for it.
I stand surrounded by my own

pick handles, postcards, coins,
sore souvenirs from all my wars.

No bargains here.
There'll be none then.

WAY OUT THERE IN RADIOLAND
(1934)

A Fada unfades in
from some where, from some when:
its amber dial alight
with number-letter towns
that stretch from WNBC-
to Nashville-Tennessee-
to WBZ-Boston-home to WSPD.
That yellow eye within its
flare of metal lip
is oracle.

We wait for miracle to warm
to come to hum, to song;
its speakermouth (oblong)
flings its soft mantle over us and—
shhhh, oh shhh, and
aaaah!
We sit back
listening.

Our day being done,
we rest, we bask,
having trapped the air called voice
and music (kind is never mind
or more or less) having caught
the ether waves inside the cone
that beams their outside messages
into our inner ears of heart and home,
having in that flowing dark
beneath that dome of sound

built dams of memories
of small-life town,
of farm, of family,
and all for free.

In our small innocence
of what the sounds are all about
we cannot see nor speak nor feel
that which is going out.

How can we know
we've plunged into a river
rolling out beyond the sun,
how can we know
the journey from ourselves
has just begun.

SNAPSHOT

(My mother takes my photograph)

Faded, gray, your shadow slants across my face,
my eyes unsmiling, blind to life
beyond the frame:

If I could call you back,
if I could kiss your lips to life
what-is-thirty-years-to-death
my mama. If I could ...
Where is Monday morning now?

Your arms uplifted in a steam of clothes,
your jaw set stiff in struggle toward a grove
of poles that slant against a winter sky,
toward snapping sheets, toward crackling
underpants as cold as steel as sharply clean;

if I could call you,
call you back to
waiting arms—
or even
automatic
wash
machine!

There's only this:
young and smiling, holding up
your small black box,
you point it at me: *click!*
You've locked me in your kodak's kiss.
I'm kneeling by your tulip bed,
my arms around our

long dead
dog.

POTATO PLANTERS

When old moon signs spoke out
and spring still seemed a chance,
my father stretched and said,
"It's time to plant." My mother
sitting on the porch step only
sweatered from the damp
sliced seed potatoes to a size
both small enough and large enough
for eyes. Waiting for his nod,
I lifted up the pail, the wire bit bone,
and off we went toward garden soil,
his hand around my own, he leaning
on his spade but touching it so lightly
on the grass, I stumbling to be quick,
my free arm beating air, a flightless chick,
the dark earth trembling as we passed.

The ground he struck was sure to be
still hard from winter cling, but
when my father turned the clay,
its fume was spring.

Behind his shovel then, I'd drop
the seed chunks raw. And if he cut
a worm in two we saw, he'd spit
and we would move along in strange
regret. I never doubted every eye
I dropped would sprout, nor when
our chunks were crop and foliage down,

we'd dig into the miracle
and wheel our harvest home.

But such sweet dusks are gone.
Half-waking in my city's dawn,
I like to dream some larger Eden lies
where she, my mother, warm and wise,
is still dividing life between its eyes,

where he, my father, turns a blade
in some bright glade of far more fertile soil
than now I know. I like to think that some cherubic child
runs with them in their night

broadcasting from celestial pails
raw miracles of light, but oh …

And yet, my father knew his moons,
my mother earths, and
I have dropped behind His spade
extraordinary deaths.

SWEET CHARIOT

(At the funeral parlor)

Spared of both his birth and death
I knew but little of my father's girth
and height. Not having to identify
the body on that night (one red mark
on the chin as if he might have nicked
himself when last he shaved), not having
heard his last goodbye, the *ooh!* (the para-
medic told me that he sighed), I doubt
that I'd have known him.
Though his hands seemed what I could recall,
without his breath without the slightest motion
even they were strangely gray.
And not of him.

              I walked away
believing he'd not really dashed
at all against that board, that
molded sponge that safe device
that took him up from all his fear
and dread.

              I walked away demanding
that he'd heard the comfort words
and gently leaned into the darkness
with his heart.

RESTORING A DUCK DECOY

I touch acrylic paint to neck, to wing,
following my father's brush, his curve of knife;
false, I daub upon a falser life that fifty years ago
bobbed Judas-like upon an Erie bay
where living wings would swoop to join
the silent flock, secure. Then Bang!
my father's gun would spit, and
dying wings would flop, would drop
into that split between two worlds.

When he came home, his jacket bulging
with the prize, he'd lay the ducks
before my wondering eyes
and all I felt was his immensity.

He'd grumble some about the limit, ten,
about the sixty dollars rent he'd paid for marsh,
he'd tell of how he'd shot a hundred in one day
when as a boy he'd hunted all across the township,
watching thousands cross the bay, darkening
the gray Ohio flyway.

And then we'd work. We'd scald them, pluck them,
sort the down, and he would tack the wings he
liked up on the coal bin door.

You old decoy, you silent quacker, riding
motionlessly on my bench, I touch you
wonderingly. You are that forgotten time
when in my innocence, my one strong man
could rise up out of blind, could strike down
living flesh for me, and I

could cry for pride, not pity,
but for pride.

COLUMBIA

(Upon hearing that shuttle debris was for sale on E-Bay, Feb. 1, 2003)

I'm very young. I'm holding father's hand,
we're running toward Mylander's field,
to where an army biplane
nosed into his corn.
Thick smoke is curling from
propeller shaft, sheered, black.
The shoulder wings
are slumped against the earth.

Around us on the ground lie
splinters, canvas shreds,
strut-wire sprawl, the air is
full of oil stink, gas,
and men are shouting,
running, shouting,
men are running
round and round.

One stops to pick up
metal strips, another
slivers,
raw.

I stoop to pick up one small stick,
but father jerks me back
and we go home.

BEING DEAD PROPERLY AS DESIGNATED AT THE ENTRANCE TO A GRAVEYARD IN OHIO

1. Floral tributes must be placed at sides of monuments.
   Mowers will not cut graves where plants are put in front of stones.

> Grim those reapers riding tractors
> roaring over only graves. If
> Tommy Hardy's mistress asked today
> about the padding of her dog above
> her head she'd never hear about the
> rue no lover dared to plant improperly
> nor even know about her poodle's bone;
> instead a Briggs and Stratton four-
> and-one-half horse would rap its rotary,
> would rop-rop-rop her RIP.

2. All persons on these premises after sundown will be
   PROSECUTED!

> After the decorators have departed
> leaving plastic roses and their VFW flags,
> the twilight touches red-winged blackbirds
> riding reeds beside the river's bend
> that curls within its legalistic arm
> the endless prosecution
> of the night.

FOR FRED

For fifty years my brother Fred embalmed
with Floyd, helping in the room behind the store.
On second floor were casket rows, on first the sofas,
loveseats, chiffoniers, linoleum rolls along the walls.
From horse and wagon on Fred drove the ambulance (the hearse)
until Floyd bought a Cadillac but he drove that himself.
Floyd waited on the trade out front while Fred laid out
the corpses in the rear, and kitchen floors.

For fifty years my brother walked to work and
home again. One wintry noon before Thanksgiving Day
he walked his alley route and felt I guess
the cramp of all the morning's squatting
in the Carstairs' kitchen laying floor.
A neighbor saw him drop into the snow
and called up Floyd. No help of course.
A young Doc Heller came and pulled a blanket
over Fred's blue face. I saw how far his bootprints got.

Flo waited at the house with wild duck
but it got cold at last, and all that time
old Floyd was reaching down to pick my brother up
without a word. I helped him slide the body
on the rack, and walked the alley route to go tell
Flo. She said she couldn't believe it,
but she put away his knife and fork.
And I went home.

Floyd had to lay him out of course and said
he guessed he'd have the flooring now to do

and was put out. That wasn't necessary, not to me,
he was my flesh and blood, you know.

So when my Clara died within the year,
I took her all the way to Alamont
to give her to a stranger's hand.
Fred might have liked the way it all turned out.
I'd say he knew.

SOCIAL NIGHT AT THE LODGE HALL

When we discovered how to work the lock,
we slid the cloakroom door into the wall
and went inside. We squeezed between thick rows
of coats and pants, our faces brushing hard
against the pricky wool, the braids
and sashes, buckles, buttons
till we pushed to where the swords
and scabbards lay upon a shelf along the wall.
Afraid to touch them but more scared
that we would not, we ran our fingers
up and down the dull steel blades,
and giggled. Then we saw the hats,
their great white feathers filling up
the shelves behind the glass, and gasped.
Out in the hall was laughter, fathers, mothers
playing cards, and in the kitchen
women making coffee, piling thick baloney slices
on the soft white bread.

These were the times when held between the
blue and gold of wool serge suits that smelled of men
and sweat no cleaner could remove, we touched
the promises of what we could become
that we had known in movies, books—kings and princes,
knights and squires. We learned the feel,
the royal weight of robes, of steel, the brush of
feathers, braids of gold. We knew that somehow
in some distant day we'd rule our own

majestic monarchies, if only in the
consumation of our secret lives.

SLEEPS

On sofa, feet apart, I dream about a child
lost in trees.

South, one hundred miles, extracted
from a car, a gray old man who'd
fathered me, is stretched out in an
ambulance beneath the wail,
the whirling red, the clear-the-way
that ferries death

The phone call comes,
but child within me will not hear
and hiding runs toward deeper trees
where deadly boughs are smashing down
like tinkered toys like rough collapse
of pickupsticks that falling sky has
thrashed across the universe.

Run! Run quick into the mouth of black
of white that sucks me toward the
rasping maw toward instant ice
that cracks in skulls that melts
in molecules in atoms split
in proton-lectron all the sagging DNA's
in red spermatic pools.

Collision, head on
Arrival, dead on

ROOFER

(1931)

She must not know I hate like hell
to roof these silo shells. My kneeshake
never stops not even overnight, not even
when I am beside her in the dark.
Even then I dream of falling forward
into sucking wheat where children
throw me inner tubes on ropes I cannot catch.
How could she, oh she must not know
what eighty, ninety feet of space
behind the heel is like.

In morning wind I hang on to my hammer
while it hangs on to to heads of nails.
In afternoon the chaff sprays film into my eyes;
too scared to wipe, I blink and blink and pound
and pound, *how can I tell her?* that I pray to live
to each day's end. How can she know how far away
the green looks changing into gray
along the river's bend. She counts on me.

She knows that when her mister's paid
it's for a man who's not afraid to climb
and does his job right. She counts on that.
I am her fact.

Don't tell me that I've got a brother-in-law
to pick his goddamned apples for a dime a crate.
Sure, he lets me roof his henhouse for ten cents
an hour while he collects his pension for the thumb
he ripped apart *before* the war—why, he was trimming

Northern Spies out in his southwest orchard. Sure!
I know the spot! Some doughboy-legionnaire-big shot,
marches Decoration Day! How can I tell her how it feels
to hang against his apple trees or spray or load his hay
or fix his coop for ninety cents a day.

She calls me roofer. So I'll be.
I'd sooner blow across the county line,
I guess, from this damned silo here,
than take that other pay.
At least I would have made the trip for something,
as they say.

TOWARD EXIT

(After reading Hans Christian Andersen's "The Staunch Tin Soldier")

In all my dreams the EXIT light is on,
not red but circled white as if
the opening to a cave or sewer
that belches into sea;

and then I tumble
lungfull up and over down around
through rush of foam and rapids
borning dying dark and light and
always just ahead a voice resounding
in the tube: *Child! Come!* and I,
I do not know nor half remember if
I am or not. Or could it be *PASSPORT!*
and I the steadfast one in paper boat
who rushes constant toward a red
oblivion of mouth. It could be
blood pulsating vein, or urine
flooding toward a toilet bowl,
or pellets swirling shot
through oily bore of barrel, it
could be … *God!*

I wake up
on the kitchen board to cook's knife
bringing light and all
the old familiar scenes of home.

If I do escape one day by fish
or other such circuitous route

we all know even staunch one ended up
in lump (albeit heart)
with love beside him (spangled yes)
but burnt as black as any coal and
just as numb.